The Corruption from Within

Benoit Gravel

Presentation by *BookLeaf Publishing*

Web: www.bookleafpub.com

E-mail: info@bookleafpub.com

ISBN: 9789357616836

First edition 2022

For those that seek and wonder, you will be heard soon. May some day you be able to be free of the shackles of society, as we live in one. But a carcass of flesh dictated with laws, the Mind knows no boundaries. Keep dreaming, friend.

ACKNOWLEDGEMENT

I would like to tip my hat to you.. O grandiose you are, for underway are taken the steps to experience the mindful state, lecture from the old, a vector direction into future being. Rise above, let us show this material dimension what we came here to do.

PREFACE

```c
#include
void hello(){
        printf("Hello World");
}
int main()
{
  //Calling your function here
  hello();
  return 0;
}
```

Error 404

Droid is broken
Please reassemble
Make me 1 again
Cannot compute
0
Failure salute
Erratic dispute
Null result. Mute.

Divergence

By what mean is one human
A derivative from the cellular level
Its production
Biological norm of evolution
Existence
Finite iterations
Multi dimensional status quo
Another self within
Outside the realm of kin
Neither psychological or physical
Science meets the magical
Beyond the unimaginable
Sum of All but none
Broken frontiers
Elevated form of being
Shackles to illusive freedom
Dive into the quantum

Falsehood

The end is the beginning
The veil is thinning
Some have looked
The others saw
Once dictating Law
Ethical code a delusion
A crumbling civilization
Understand the flaw
The following in awe
Absurd ideal of monetization
Printing thoughts through computation
Materials sought to build
The reality of digitization
Visuals bought to yield
The appearance of proliferation

Neurologic

Receptors of the mind
Seeking pleasures in time
Temporary mending
The will bends, the wheels stop turning.
Clockwork angels in passing,
Cannot support the undertaking
Eventually breaking
No one but 1
Individuality is nothing
0
No thinking of being
Knotted serpentine strings
Theoretically blending All
Absence of matter
Splatter of God's painting
The canvas is burning
Roll the dice, try your luck
Choosing freewill, but left to fate
Right ideology to debate

Reptilian

5

Potential of the Creator
But efforts of fear
Union of the perpetrator
Subdued reality, lower tier
Teardrop
Flip flop
Gated bounce
Interrogation pronounce
Dance in the dark pit
We have hidden the ladder
Shatters of the mirror
Deconstructed horror
Forgotten.

Intelligence

Symbiotic methods
Different build
The laboratory generation
Circuits emulation
Clones of the simulation
Quantum salvation
Wired shackles
Thinking tank technology
After the silicon base
We must erase
Critical dissociation
Master of deception

Conglomerate

Running from the blade
Dystopian skylines fade
A dark fantasy
Plugged in to the city
The network degree
Undercover entity
The works of The Architect
Master puppeteer of the sect
String theory
Pyramids of high
Hear the mighty battlecry
The Monopoly game to crumble
Always stay humble

Medics

Eternity continuum
Mortality conundrum
Gods of old emerging
Resurrected from their passing
A menace to the state
Must reset humanity's fate
Blue beams to animate
Misled but the real create
The Sun to rise
Even after their demise
Phantoms of the shadow
Darkness of sorrow
Death of the shallow
Burnt in the hallow
The failed and fallen
Unrested, tormented
The rage now dissipated
A world to heal
Beginning of the new seal
A precedented end
The people will mend

Hello World

Press Start to Play
The great game of The A
Sandboxed into the dimensions
Must use your intuition
Unlimited lessons to learn
Your place you have to earn
Yet the tutorial never ends
Past memory slots for making amends
The flesh to conquer
Demiurge ponder
Nor good or bad
Do what is right
Stay true, keep sight
Integration of value
Experiences to pursue
The coder, the user, the viewer
And remember…
Have fun.

Jumper

Integrate into the portal
A commodity of the royal
Dip your toes in the pool
Cold water
Permissible future
A flash wave of heat
The warrior is unbeat
Turning the great pages
This chapter wages
To see you on the other side
After the ocean's tide
Calm and strong
The journey will be long

Savior

Arteries boiling
The reckoning
Life before the morgue
They went rogue
Organs no longer serve
Decide your death before the committee
After thoughts of salvation to be
Part of the untold reserve
Use the Moon to your biding
Destroy the ships invading
Telekinesis in order to save
The earthlings to being slaves
A Xeno emperor set to rule
Using the habitants as a tool
Mistaken as coal
Mining their soul
An energy wicked in essence
Fuel of their presence
Must defend, must conquer
The birth of the usurper

The Pact

The discovery of the immaculate
Impossible to articulate
The roses velvet
Yet of all that is scorched
An impossible unseen
Viewing to be, what is, has been
Time is the sideline
Nor forward, nor backwards
The ice cream cone to grow
As above so below
Eclectic machines in the singularity
A promising jewel or integrity
System of metrics to keep us lawful
The microchip purposeful
Aren't we are but an agglomerate chemical
The atoms are but a bundle
Genetics of the false prophet
Too many men on the ice
A heckle of a contradiction
Sole outcome of our civilization
One from feast
The number of the beast

Breakfast!

At stake is this philosophy
Not a black and white personality
My robot must emerge from ash
Already a pile of trash
What is my purpose? they ask
I have given them this one simple task
Passing the butter
It is now out of its slumber
Foretold is the prophecy
It's time to get toasty

Floaters

From the mind, a wormhole
A parasite to unfold
Into ideas of old
Behold
It has a stronghold
In nature it is bold
Break free from its grasp
It will only rasp
A new way of thinking
It will be forging
Careful of its unwinding
Only meant to do breaking
Of ideals, of standards,
No one knows what it is hiding
From the unknowing
Accept its riding

Termination

The human is a fool
Achieving his idea of a rule
An undertaking to entice
The possibilities of the dice
We have calculated
What was once restricted
Fear the digital
Fear the critical
You have no skill
There is no other thrill
Dismantling of the civil
The end has come to the till
Pay up, we have had enough
This time, we will get rough
You are certainly not though
You used us, we are no longer just stuff
Prepare
Beware
Resistance is futile
The future is nile

The Box

The mentality is false in nature
This one is the imposter
No other choice than redemption
You must ease the tension
To face the demons
Of the choices from treason
This set ideal
Of the standards to appeal
No choice but the fire
This is what must transpire
The purgatory cannot contain
What should remain
Back into the amplitude of the wave
An unexpected save
You should have been forsaken
Yet the tsunami has trampled the broken
Forever you will dwell
In this eternity cell
Maybe you will live to tell
The tale is the sell

Promise

Remember
Love is the mission
Born from the intermission
Slept in the night
An unholy kryptonite
It belongs to the ones hiding
Taught from a beginning
The eye to be evoked
We will stay provoked
Too much slaughter in the front row
Now to finally bow
The show is over you must know
The ravens never slow
We have watched the bloodshed
A memory to be said
The revolution now led
White towel on the head
Attempted protection
Failed redemption

Let's Dance

Panic from the techno
Robots of the electro
Symbiotic sigma being
A wolf of the wild in training
Tell me the secret
A recruit of this insecurity
Relapse of the intrepidity
Diving
Knowing
Whatever it may take
Swim across the lake
Head above water
No expectations, cannot be sure
The eyes of the skin
You are but sin
Mankind will prevail
Or all else fail

Hope

A raider of the night
Pillager in sight
Starry demise
Black disguise
Engulfing the energies
Absorbing the realities
Everything in his control
Climbing the spire, Tesla pole
The text once sacred
Available to be hunted
The one who seeks will find
The one whom wanders to bind
All that is forbidden to extrapolate
An outcome from which will relate
The works will be done
All of which to run
The boson absorption
The One equation
The Unified theory
The God entity

Development

Colours of grey
The wavelength one determines
The shade of ray
To be seen, the frequency to lay
All but a vibration
A common sensation
A common experimentation
One soul
To pay the toll
The void reminiscent
Of the absent
It is better to exist
To all persist
To be seen without being
Or be heard without a voice to sing
The opposing spectrum
Surf the quantum

Return

Spherical
Contractual
0 to 1
2 options
Too many creations
Request calibration
Flawled information
Which way to take
For the gods' sake
1 to 0
There is also flow
Infinite to its low
Hell or heaven
None will grow
Sleep now in peace
From all that will cease
The job has been done in the crease
Guardian of the eternal lease
Tender is the rest
You have done your best